T0198639

Ascension

A Poetic Chronicle In Progress Vol.1

CHARLES A. BARNER

authorHOUSE®

AuthorHouse™
1663 Liberty Drive
Bloomington, IN 47403
www.authorhouse.com
Phone: 1 (800) 839-8640

Published by AuthorHouse   01/22/2018

ISBN: 978-1-5462-2473-0 (sc)
ISBN: 978-1-5462-2471-6 (hc)
ISBN: 978-1-5462-2472-3 (e)

Library of Congress Control Number: 2018900530

Contents

Preface

Charles A. Barner
(A Man of God)

Here I am, yes A Man Of God who literally and disobediently turned his back on Jehovah. Yes due to the pain of rejection I gave up on enjoying God's Gift to me (life) and instead put my focus on pleasing other people and I lost sight of what is pleasing in the Eyes Of Jehovah. That is to stay focused on my daily needs, my desires and objectives and then and only then should I try to please others on a human level. So due to an inherent short-sightedness and ignorance, relative to life and humanity in general and because I was hurt more severely than most due to my physiological condition, this pain affected me harder exponentially. I did not understand how to stop a pain of excruciating proportions and I had no available means of relief and since the ones I really loved and trusted hurt me the most, I withdrew from the real world. They did not or could not understand my situation or needs.

They instead pursued the feeling, attentions and social affiliations which gave then the most pleasure and gratification on a human level. I now realize that that was a normal human trait.

I was experiencing a physiological state of nervous pain, brought on by a childhood inflicted injury (neighborhood youth) and it causes me extreme fluctuating periodic pain and discomfort, to this very day. Being inherent, modern medicine could not cure it due to my limited financial resources and relative family circumstances, at that time, I therefore became spiritually, mentally and physiologically coaxed and motivated to pursue a curative or other soother that would keep the debilitation at bay or cause it to be completely eradicated. So in fairness to all past acquaintances who shared some of their life force with me, I say thank you and May God Bless You and I hope to repay you for your shared love and kindness multiplied many times. This set the stage for my research and development of what I call The Embryonic Elixir Of Healing.

Due to the degree of debilitating pain, physiologically and not being a medical practitioner, I did not know how to relay to others my impairment without seeming to be asking for sympathy, pity, special treatment or ostracism due to a general misunderstanding of my condition. Reluctantly, I retreated into a world of excuses and sorrow and I tried to extricate myself from a world of insensitivity, cruelty and reality. The problem, I discovered, was that as a living human being, my presence still affected all those individuals who I came into contact with whether verbally, physiologically, emotionally or spiritually. So as a man in search of a realistic, strong connection with our Heavenly Father, I have accepted His Holy Name as Jehovah God and I am pursuing my passion for His Holy Word. As a home study student of theology, related church doctrines I will merge this study pursuit with my ample background in technological fields of study (mechanical engineering, math, drafting, graphics, promotion and productions), so as to obtain a sound, concise understanding of the relationship between God, mankind, the universe and technology.

My purpose will be to develop a way of thinking which will instill within me a pathway of living for myself and all like minded individuals. By way of a formative thought process, I have conceived a positive way of living formula which I have initiated and labeled p12max5, which is literally expressed as positive living to the max to the fifth power (prayer, peace, promotion, power and prosperity). In short, Serenity, a positive, prosperous and spiritual way of living.

In search of a way of life which would be a stabilizing force in society for myself as well as people from the diverse segments of other respecting communities, I have studied and gained invaluable experience in the areas of singing, modeling, dancing, fashion, public relations, I have developed a fairly accurate sense of what related services, goods and products would do well in terms of sales to the general public.

At this point I feel compelled to relate my whole track physiological experiences and what sensations caused me to pursue a cure or relative soothers for my daily aches and pains. As the result of an unfortunate destabilizing incident at the age of 8 (a fracture within my lower extremities by a neighborhood youth, my body went through a whole series of contorted traumas. I went through paralysis, medical treatment, a leg brace and even extended periods of hospitalization. Nothing corrected my condition so for the next 3 years (ages 8-11) I experienced what I consider to have been my own hell on earth. It was a sentence worse than death. There was no money to buy any extra simple pleasures to quell my daily excruciating pains and anxieties, people laughed at me and found humor in my situation and basic everyday human perks escaped me and at times even my will to live was unnaturally demoralized. Yet my first miracle occurred.

A spiritual spark ignited my soul and my spirit became inflamed with a power that can only be described as supernatural and my spirit evolved and seemed to become an entity of a separate living personage. An inherent ability to suppress the pain began to emerge and although my nerves were overly intoxicated, my ability to move about became easier and my normal degree of mobility returned. Now even though I could perform most normal chores and tasks my case doctors told me and my grandmother that there wasn't much that they could do to correct my impairment so they told me to think positive, and maybe, in the future a remedy would present itself. Not that they didn't try to help me, it just happened that I was a victim of circumstances (at birth) and I will always carry a special blessing in my heart for all those physicians who helped me during those years of youthful struggle and conflict. I now know that experience is what caused me to call upon The Power of Our Heavenly Father that is inherent in all of us. It was not a medical practice to use faith and holistic healing as a means of physiological treatment for physical injuries. No one knew (1962-1965) that even a child could be taught how to develop a healing connection between the mind, body and soul and thus cause a healing reaction within the body. It's not that pastors, ministers and other duly authorized clergy do not understand the power of prayer but I have found that faith is proportionately effective based on the mental aptitude of the respective person in question. For instance a child of 2 years of age could hardly be expected to fully understand the terminologies of the written word whether it be on a general academic level of his/her peers no more than he or she could read and learn and understand the bible, comprehend it's meaning and then inherently know how to apply it to their life for beneficial guidance, strength and healing in times of sickness, confusion or trouble. I had to learn for myself that the spirit could incite the body's immune system and healing properties to kick in and cause metaphysical stimulations in one's body. This combined with the power or will to survive (faith) may in fact be a whole other field of healing that I believe should be investigated (by the time my book is published I believe this will be a known fact and be a practiced norm). Not that my situation was a rarity but I believe my case doctors had no idea that I could become a productive member of society.

Now here's the absolute, unimaginable, spiritual twist. At age 9, I began developing my own personal program of healing. I prayed daily (3 times). I stretched at home (isometrics) at regular intervals, I applied personal body massages on my muscles and joints, I played basketball and exercised in the park (2-4 hours/per day)/ 3-5 times/wk, more in the summertime, I walked, jogged and ran (2-4 hrs/day, 3-5 times a week, more in the summertime. This also increased my lung capacity and my blood oxygenation. My overall physical strength increased. The extra breathing helped me concentrate better. I began reading about herbs and vitamins and I included fruits and vegetable in my daily diet. I drank regular servings of milk (for strong bones and teeth), I attended regular Sunday school classes and church, I meditated every day (various times periods) and last but not least, I had an extremely healthy, positive home life which I attribute to my grandmother (Alverta Thrasher). She had an extremely high and rare understanding of God and was honest, fair and loving, God rest her soul.

All of the aforementioned aspects of my life, incorporated with personal faith and study of God's Word, are what I believe caused an unexpected physiological curation to occur. Even though the aches and pains continued, as time went on, my mental concentration grew stronger, faster and more focused. My ability to walk normally (ages 11-12) grew steadily and I could maintain the energy to handle chores and tasks without concerted effort. I incorporated the herbs and vitamins I studied into my daily diet and daily routine. I meditated and prayed regularly and thus became a well-balanced mental, physical and spiritual person. I therefore believe that as I grew up, my daily regimen of good habits, good diet, prayer and meditation contributed to a pretty much well-balanced stable physiology and very happy life-style.

At this point, I must reassert that having a supportive pleasant advisor/ caretaker, my grandmother – Alverta Thrasher, was probably the best medicine (literally) I could have been blessed with. She allowed me to develop my own opinions about life and she therefore allowed me to be myself. Good or bad, right or wrong she set a positive example for me and this is where my natural affinity towards God, the desire to help other and a positive outlook towards the future comes from. It resides in me, at present and I crave it's full redevelopment and sustenance. Next to a sound, healthy, spiritual cognition of Our Heavenly Father (Jehovah God), I unequivocally believe that self-confidence, education and accumulated wisdom are what allowed me to become a sound, respectful person between the ages 14-20.

Now even though my reeducation about life, people and those elements of survival which were above the human norm (universal quantifications), I still needed a reachable set of goals that were a bit more practical and attainable on a level that people could relate to and achieve on a timetable suitable to their resources and personal time availability. I thus became engrossed in social group productions I felt I should pursue personal physical training with health as an initial priority.

I undertook a personal empowerment program (1970-1974) by which I became agile and healthy enough to run a mile in 5 minutes + 30 seconds I could leg press up to 750lbs (4 sets of 188) at a body weight of 135 lbs, I graduated high school with honors and went on to college and was able to study a college mechanical engineering curriculum 5 days a week (14 hrs a day) for my first two years. Now here is the point of my dismay. My debilitation, being ever present, seemed to pop up at inappropriate times and them, as an accumulative effect my powers of concentration and application seemed to become proportionately compromised and highly depleted. I was greatly discouraged and gave up on ever the smallest pleasures in life. I also became susceptible to unhappiness, disappointment and the effects of jealousy, hatred, degradation, suppression and all forms of emotional, mental and physical attacks, projected at me from the members of society who wished harm and misfortune upon me.

In spite of this proportionate public opposition, I focused on the positive support given to me by supportive family members and like-minded associates. My primary goal, in life, is to be healthy, wealthy and wise. My thinking will be governed by the infusion of prayer, meditation, study and application.

In search of a way of life which would be stable and at the same time beneficial to myself, affiliated members of my family and society as well, I have studied a few forms of expression and I feel that I have reached a proficient degree of mathematics, artistic application (graphics) and literary expression. I feel very confident that the pursuit of business projects and community programs correlated in a group format could be very feasible, enjoyable and a rewarding path to pursue. Some related forms to pursue would be show production and interrelated group and individual training via modeling, singing, dancing, poetry and the performing arts.

In preparation for becoming a qualified individual who can bring quality presentations to the general public, I have accumulated approximately 106 credits towards an engineering degree (mechanical) from NJIT, Newark, New Jersey. I have 2 years substitute math teaching experience (East Orange, New Jersey). I have 42 years of talent, modeling, fashion show production experience, I have 1 patented invention (A Social Dome/A modular Home (10/12/2000), as well as my own fashion line aptly named Bourgeoisle'. I have been graphically designing fashions since 1980, I have 291/2 years of fast food service experience and I served on my city's (Orange, N, J.) citizen budget advisory committee for 2 years. I, therefore feel that I have a pretty well rounded hands on production background as to how to go about putting beneficial programs and projects together. I shall pursue this quest with the utmost vim and vigor. I will also take refresher courses in related background areas as well as present day suggested areas of study (e-mails, basic computers, basic and advanced mechanical engineering and business management courses.

As but one spiritual avatar incensed with a desire for promotion, and production proficiency, I am ambitiously looking to hone my mentality, my intellectual abilities and relative senses. I am striving to regain clear cognition, intuitiveness, premonition, inner vision, introspection, keen comprehension and understanding and enhanced perception. I thus believe that as a result of regaining a strong, healthy, agile mind, body and soul inundated with senses advanced, heightened and spiritually endowed with more than enough energy and power to undertake the rigorous schedule which I feel I will have to adhere to in order to achieve the life mission I believe God has set before me. I pledge to do my best in all related endeavors and when the day comes when have become what I strive to be, I shall emit a sound of glorious celebration and it shall be heard to heights unbounded. Heart be strong and resilient and May I Dwell In The House Of Our Father Jehovah God On Earth As It Is In Heaven.

I, therefore affirm and attest that, as a poet, writer, graphics artist, graphics-fashion designer, promoter, producer and concerned citizen of community affairs, I am extremely adamant about the positive progress of society. I sincerely hope to make a lasting impression on the general public. I intend to initiate a full body healing and sharpen all of my abilities and skills to such a high degree of mastery so that with the necessary guidance and support, all related projects, programs and shows would meet and surpass all duly proposed guidelines mandated by related business criteria and city, state, federal agencies and affiliated offices. I also believe that a platform of international proportions will develop if all related parties meet required standards.

I am intent on making it my life's work of being an asset to society, my aim will be to become mature, credible, honest, intelligent, respectful and spiritual. I shall use these qualities to remember that unity comes about thru the accurate understanding that worthy people need to retain their integrity and freedom of choice when it comes to their choice of direction and purpose in life.

When it comes to darkness, despair, sickness, doubt, confusion, fear or just an uneasy feeling of loneliness, each person has a vast army of bible verses to turn to for a shining light thru their space related storm of spiritual doom whether thru imposed public suppression or personal subjection (extreme sickness, overwhelming financial distress or civil unrest), just to name a few examples. I also discovered that to be truly effective I have found that a person that is verifiably educated and skilled in spiritual or church doctrines should be consulted when a person is in need of help when confronted with problems that they themselves just don't understand or know how to cope with. If allowed to persist for too long a period of time said circumstance or condition could lead to sickness, neurosis or death. This is my opinion and should not be compared to or treated as any form of medical diagnosis. An effective daily helpful suggestion for having a peaceful, healthy mental attitude is to have a positive outlook on life, be around people who you trust, have good feelings for and incorporate some form of study of God's Word as a daily literal routine. A positive mental attitude combined with good self-esteem can be a wonderful ingredient to help a person feel empowered and good about themselves. These are but a few things that worked for me but I stress that each individual can develop his/her own value system and gain valuable experience getting to truly know themselves. Even though it is best to have a home life where one's greatest support system does initially come from but I have found this is not the case in every home so outside support is always a good option or addition i.e. a relative neighbor, a close friend, a teacher, a guidance counselor, a barber, a community program counselor, a pastor/minister or church officer or other trusted professional personal contact. You can choose for yourself and I suggest you pray on it and use sound judgement.

In past times of disappointment, heartbreak, sickness, confusion and sometimes just for relaxation I have read the 23rd Psalms, The Book of Job, The Serenity Prayer and Footprints In The Sand and are but four bible verses that have worked for me. They are always there and will help you find your way to personal glory after all the Word of God is everlasting and God does not fail or make mistakes.

I hope my life experiences reach anyone who has been at points in the dark life where they just didn't know what to do and so they buried any hope of resolution in conformity. Yes they accepted that things of a beneficial nature just weren't meant for them so they gave up and never found that God given illumination is residing in their soul. What as well I'm here to do is cause a spark of motivation within anyone who is courageous enough to defy the odds and pick up their mantle of ambition & faith and once again walk the walk of faith on the pathway of positivity. Yes let's seek each other in brotherhood and combine our efforts to achieve all our collective goals and see if what we perceive can become a mutual goal. My personal business goal is The Rise Complex. I would love to meet and greet you and discuss your goals and May Our Father Bless Us Till we meet in person.

I have included my present calendar of future construction projects, goals and objectives.

Construction Chronology

As but one individual who has persevered through sickness, hardship, pain, jealousy, darkness, betrayal, envy, self-denial and miscommunication with Our Heavenly Father (Jehovah). I now attest that without The Love From God, Jesus And The Holy Ghost and my acceptance of Their Love and then the return of my personal love back to them, my spiritual restoration would not have been possible. Yes only thru study, understanding and application of The Word of God, my obedience to His Word in my development of a true, accurate and realistic bond with The Father, The Son and The Ghost, can true peace, power and prosperity, for me, be obtained. Yes for anyone to seek, obeyand also maintain a life of pleasure, happiness and well-being, seek ye first The Kingdom Of God and all things you desire and work for will manifest themselves here on earth.

It has been a labor of love, healing as well as a great pleasure to serve but one spiritual channel to convey to all who share my zest for life, that you must never forget that as a human being, created by God, you must cherish His Gift Of Life, to you and 1st, last and forevermore your gift back to Him is to be the best that you can be. As it is written and spoken keep your eyes on the sparrow as a symbol of freedom and hope for a better tomorrow. I've learned for myself & since this is a truism of life I respectfully ask and pray that you at least give it a try. So, as an expression of literary submission recommend that we should all obey The Word Of God, abide and obey The Laws Of Mankind and we all will be protected, respected and credible In The Name Of The Father, The Son And The Holy Ghost, these things I pray. Amen and Amen!

Introduction

I've been on a journey, through life, for 54 years but just now have I received the perspicacious comprehension to understand my mission in life. I have written this book as a guide to anyone seeking a poetic direction, for expressions and a surefire reachable literary objective. I have spent 27 years writing Ascension.

Ascension is an ongoing literary project that I feel best allows me to express my ideals and feelings in a positive way. It is a book that will give insights into my creative realm which I have kept private and personal, so as not to be too open and trusting in today's complicated, cruel and harsh world. It was a place to which I could travel, at will and feel safe, secure and fully exposed without fear of reprisal from negative rebuttal whether it be verbal or physical in nature.

So many times a person may feel trapped on pent up and will thus turn off or tune out from the real world. Their problems pile up and without a vent or release, transform into a neurosis and then if untreated, develops into anxiety, phobias or depression. The end result is many times a mental illness or worse.

I therefore assert that my book, Ascension, is to inspire others as proof positive that with enough positive reinforcement, prayer, a healthy lifestyle, good eating habits, regular exercise, sound medical advice and treatment, I firmly believe that anyone can overcome the negativity associated with everyday trials and tribulations. Instead people can call upon the forces of good and allow these productive forces to be the guiding light in their lives.

My main concern, for writing Ascension, is to inspire as many people as possible, to pursue whatever positive creative outlets they may have. Never think that no one is interested in your ideas, dreams, and aspirations or plans as long as they are constructive, progressive and beneficial to society, whether it is on local, city, and state, national or international level.

I must relate that, Ascension, is but one segment of my journey and with your assistance, I strive to be a force of positivity. I firmly believe our creator has inspired me to use my gift of expression to relay his message of peace and prosperity. His message is that with love for him (Jehovah God), love for thyself and love for others, all of our spiritual talents will be manifested on the human plane, of existence and truly transform thisplanet into the treasure that he truly intended it to be.

I hope to touch as many people as possible with Ascension. I truly enjoyed writing it and firmly believe that most everyone will find some poetry which they can relate to and enjoy. I will continue to write as many editions, as possible and I invite all talented poets, writers, publishers and the community at large, to join this project and help me give, to Jehovah, a masterpiece that will show our love and respect for him. I respectfully request your input and support.

My Mission On Earth

By Charles A. Barner

10/15/02

RISE – Resort & Business, Education & Entertainment Complex

Introduction

In the winter of 1990, while meditating and trying to relax, I felt a sudden urge to begin drawing. I did not know what was pulling at me, but I felt an undeniable sense of inspiration. I began at the center of the page and began to layout a concentric drawing. Keeping in mind past inspired drawings, I incorporated, "A Social Dome / A Modular Home" as well as A Rest and Comfort Station" into this drawing. While remembering previous related scaled drawings, I produced a drawing which seems to represent a scaled city or future housing community.

Due to overall related building considerations, required funding needs and land area requirements, it seems to represent a final projected building project which I have been inspired to present to interested professionals or supportive individuals for a possible future building project.

This represents a complex that would give all future investors a definite concise project that would be worthy of all concerted efforts and financial support combined with organizational finance and community input (city, State, national & international), required for its completion.

It will be a project that all involved participants would never become tired or bored with. In lieu of the projected funding, physical labor and ongoing coordination needed, I seriously doubt that I would or will see its completion in my lifetime.

I retrospectively believe that by manifesting the required mental energy, spirituality, business acumen and group support, for its completion, I feel inspired to introduce to mankind what may indeed become, with **God's Blessing**, "The Next Wonder Of The World."

Rise Complex

Day Perspective
(Daytime View)

5

Dedication

In loving memory, I am dedicating this book to my grandmother Alverta Thrasher, who taught me the true meaning of faith and perseverance. As a youngster, beset with unimaginable problems and circumstances, she instilled within me the spiritualstrength to deal with life and always give respect to our heavenly father. I have come to know him as Jehovah God and for me he's the answer to all my problems. He's the catalyst yet, we, each in our own time must seek the medical, educational, business and spiritual healing and help required to achieve our goals in life.

When required, each of us must be able to make the decision to be accountable for our mistakes, then move on with our lives and become balanced, healthy individuals and hope to obtain our optimum state of existence.

It may have taken me a lifetime, to understand her daily teachings but I've finally got it. You can only do your best if you assert yourself, pray and be honest in your dealings with people whether in personal or business situations. Yourfirst real responsibility is to be mature enough to face your adversities, be a caretaker for the sick and elderly, when required and if along the way you touch or influence someone, that's a blessing. To focus on your own life is first and foremost, everyone else's life responsibility is under divine control.

There are so many people, who have helped me in my life, that I could never give them their due credit. Therefore to all my supporters, family, friends and associates, I pledge my gratitude. I also endeavor to never forget that together we shall be a positive force in society.

I further pledge that whenever sustained prosperity enters my life, I will become a beacon to help those in need, especially all of you who were there for me as I grew and developed into the spiritual soldier commissioned by Jehovah God. I say to you let us seek each other out to re-unite in a glorious fashion unseen for a long time. If we can come together and remain united in the name of Jehovah God, Jesus Christ and the Holy Spirit, we will set a precedent that will be heard around the world. I look forward to the occasion.

In closing, I assert and affirm, that the task set before me, by Jehovah God, shall one day become a reality. I believe that by generating and maintaining the combined spiritual, mental and physical energy and skill along with the business acumen and financial support required, this monument will serve as our tribute to our spiritual father (Jehovah God) and will also provide a foundation upon which our lasting, joint wealth and prosperity will be built and endure for years to come. I have entitled this monument "Rise – Education, Business and Entertainment Complex" and I hope to see it's completion in my lifetime.

May Jehovah God bless you and be with you always. I wish you love, peace and prosperity.

Your spiritual brother,
Charles A. Barner

Acknowledgements

I have so many people to thank, in the preparation of Ascension, however it goes without saying, that unequivocally our heavenly father (Jehovah God), is the first and foremost being to whom I give my respect and credit to. All of my aspirations come from pursuit of understanding God's holy word, then being true to myself and finally striving to be the most competent human being possible and thus being an asset to society.

I also must once again thank my grandmother, Alverta Thrasher, who taught me how to be spiritual as a youngster. Her teachings guide me today. I hope to come to know Jehovah God as well as she did. I know she is with him, in spirit and I shall begin and maintain a spiritual family legacy that I know she would be proud of.

My first regimen of bible study began at the age of about 6 years old, under Rev. Norman S. G. Sr. and while entering ministerial training at age 8, my true life's path was not clear to me at the time. I thank God for Rev. G. and give him the utmost respect for what he taught me and exposed me to. While experiencing my hardest physiological trials and tribulations, he instilled in me the desire to pursue the word of God. This set a precedent within me that still exists today. I will never forget what he stood for.

As a youngster, about age 4, I became aware of a humanitarian named Mr. Melvin S. He was what I have come to know a father's father because he always seemed to make time for me at the lowest times in my life. He watched over me through the good times and the bad times and even when he reprimanded me, it was for my own good. To have known him as a personal and educational advisor was an honor indeed. I have inherited his love of children and will always feel close and connected to him. I will always cherish his memory and if I can achieve even a miniscule amount of good, as he did, I will feel I lived up to his confidence in me.

While growing into adolescence and you manhood I came upon several excursions which put me in a quandary. During a few of these excursions I had the good fortune to meet a gentleman who I would definitely say is a man amongst men. He carries what I consider an unmistakable unbreakable personality. He tried to instill in me the strength of character to face adversity, overcome it and proceed in life with confidence and tenacity. All things considered and with a littlehelp from my fellow man, I feel I will achieve all the goals he encouraged me to reach and then some. So I say to Mr. John P., here's to a job well done. Not just for what you have done for me but also for all the young people in our joint families and beyond. God bless you sir and I wish you all luck and prosperity that you so justly deserve.

At the ages of 18 – 24, I had the good fortune to attend college at NCE/NJIT. This institution allowed me to attend classes and pursue higher education which has laid the foundation for my present level of understanding and application of mechanical engineering theory, application and its use in everyday life. In spite of falling short, of my degree, I know that what I learned is invaluable. Having been apart of your educational community, sometimes disappointment resurfaces but onlybecause I was given a chance to educate myself and my degree completion has not been achieved. I say God bless all of the professors, staff and administration at NCE/NJIT and if my life's work helps others, I'll still feel empowered. I'll do my best to be worthy of your help and wish the best for all who grace the halls of the institution. I'm forever grateful. Thank you.

I have known loneliness, poverty, pain and sometimes pleasure but I believe we all need at least one person to listen to our problems and concerns. I have been extremely fortunate to have had a individual who has stuck with me, through the ups and the downs, through all my periods of alternating luck while having enough personal fortitude to be his own person. I have called him many things in the past and present but the best title I can give him is – a true friend. His name is Barry B. P. and if my life becomes even a modicum of what's projected, I will be there for him as he has been there for me. This friendship has lasted 52 years and hopefully 52 more.

While rebuilding my life and getting back on track, I needed help to regain my professional credibility and one individual stepped up and gave me a personal helping hand. His name is Mr. Kenny M. and he is like a brother to me. I do not talk to or see him much but I must give him his due credit. He's intelligent, professional, dignified and an extremely good role model. As a lifelong friend, I hope he's well and wish the best for him and his family with continued blessings.

I have come to understand that while in the pursuit of accurate bible knowledge, we sometimes need a spiritual recharge. While at my lowest spiritual ebb, a man of god visited me and gave me back the spiritual will and mental tenaciousness to face the adversities in life. This man was Rev. Harry L. B. and he was the instrument of god who delivered me from evil and helped restore my soul. Instead of feeling sorry for myself, I cleansed my mind, body and soul and picked up my mantled and I decided to pursue my life goals. He may not be here for me to confide in but he set me back on the path to divine inspiration and his confidence will not be betrayed. I pledge to never give up and strive to help others as he helped me.

As a gesture of promoting family togetherness and motivating those who have been there for me, I am giving a well deserved "Hail Mary" to an individual who gives and gives and gives. This person is my older sister Denise B. She has a peculiar sense of loyalty, mostly to her grandchildren but also to her children and she none theless showers them with unconditional love.

This is what family is supposed to be about. I have decided to pursue competence, stability and prosperity and be supportive of her and her offspring as they have been supportive of me. They embraced me when most people turned their backs on me and dismissed me as a failure. I have come to know emphatically, that when even 1 person has confidence, in you and you believe in yourself, your goals can be achieved.

As I bring this acknowledgement to close, I must give credit, of a propitious nature, to Mr. Eugene Y., who is The President of the A. C. Center, in O, N.J. He has proven to be an extremely astute businessman, a humanitarian and a prolific associate. He helps me, as he so judiciously helps all his clients and makes me believe in the fellowship of man. He was instrumental in the publication of this book and I pledge to return his aid in spades.

If I overlooked anyone, it is unintentional and everyone connected to this book shall be acknowledged in due time. I look forward to hearing from you.

With A Song In My Heart

When God shed his grace upon me
He smiled because he knew
My essence began to emanate
With a song in my heart

When I became a spirit
And my being craved to be
I realized my purpose
With a song in my heart

At the point of my conception
As I was thrust within the world
I realized my compassion
With a song in my heart

As I approached every day
Confronting all doubts
My thoughts were never shaken
With a song in my heart

At the end of each day
As I kneel my head in prayer
I give thanks to the lord
With a song in my heart

AS I experienced my life
And achieved every goal
I looked to the high heavens
With a song in my heart

When God calls me home
I'll rejoice from my soul
And give praise that he loved me
With a song in my heart

1

I Kept On Walking

When I was but a thought
And not even alive
I was nurtured by God
And I kept on walking

As the years passed by me
And my wisdom increased
I was inspired by the fact
That I kept on walking

As I progressed through my life
Just Doing my part
I'm joyous of the fact, that
I kept on walking

At the end of my day
When my thoughts commence to impart
I'm thankful for the fact
That I kept on walking

When my life on this earth
Comes to an end
I'll be grateful in my spirit
That I kept on walking

Let Go And Let God

A Poem of Faith

God is love
God is the way
So walk in hi light
Day by day

He's in every shadow
He's in every crack
When you're following <u>JEHOVAH</u>
You should never look back

(8/2/2006)

The Magic's In You

A Poem for Whitney

You May Not Know Me
But I'm Familiar With Your Life
Once Filled With Happiness
Now Sickness And Strive

Though Some May Wonder
If The Diva Is Through
I Disagree
Because The Magic's In You

Many Will Dessert You
Gossip And Scorn
All They See Is A Shell
Broken And Forlorn

But Hark To The Heavens
Where Angels Sing
And Regain Your Magesty
With The Songs You Bring

My Message Some Say
Won't Help Bring You Through
But Whitney, My Dear
The Magic's In You

Closer Than Most

One night I had a dream
For no apparent reason
I don't remember the day
Or even the season

I thought about my life
And all I lost along the way
That fine young thing
Way back in the day

Instead of remorsing
And crying in vain
I put my head to the sky
And decided to live again

I'm my own best friend
I've got family to boot
God given talent
With vibrant youth

So when times get tough
I don't brag or boast
Cause when it comes to family
We're Closer Than Most!!!

Believe It

Sometimes I sit and wonder
If my minds an empty tool
My heart is full of sadness
I feel like such a fool

I believe that she is out there
Just waiting to announce
I love you darling baby
How much I can't pronounce

I'm asking for your loving although It hurts so much
Whenever I think about you
I'm craving for your touch

So if you believe I love you
The prize will be worth the wait
What I have inside me
Is destined for your fate

So I'll just keep on waiting
And growing every day
Until she just steps up and says...
I love you in every way

<u>Grandmother</u>

When I was just a youngster
And didn't know what to do
I had a grandmother
Yes, It's true, It's true

You know
She was always the person
When everyone else said "No"
She would always say yes
An then smile a pro

When I was being bad
And my eyes would fill with tears
She would be right there for me
And wash away my fears

As I grew up to manhood
Without understanding her views
She allowed me the freedom
Yes, The ability to choose

Although quite often
I made terrible mistakes
She was always right there behind me
For goodness sake

So the next time you're shaken
And don't trust any other
Thank God for that Queen
Grandmother, Grandmother

The Midas Touch

A Poem About Prosperity
I was lounging at home
And checking out the weather
I kept thinking about my people
And when we'd be getting back together

I just had to share the news of the impending prosperity
Things were looking better
With no chance of severity

Everything has begun to glow
With favor from above
You know we're a good fit
Like a hand in a glove

What you've given me is priceless
And without hesitation
I will give you back my best
With respect and adoration

Without forgetting to honor
Our Father above
Let's continue to praise him
With motivation and love

In closing this passage
What I thought was just luck
Without the shadow of doubt
It's The Midas Touch

Unbridled Passion

Have you ever felt the need
To have something to keep
Something just yours
Where feelings run deep

It's the innermost island
With desire so rare
An area of the heart
That your passion won't share

As you journey through life
And you're ready to sire
All the things in the world
That you truly desire

That gem of a person
Who brightens your day
They make you feel special
With the eloquence that they say

Someone to depend on
Who's there to the end
They will be right there for you
Thru thick and thru thin

When the world beats you down
And you say enough is enough
Your mate's Unbridled Passion
Says never give up!!!

That's Nice

A Poem of Family Love
There are lots of things
That are good to have
But love, children and a wife
Now, that's nice, that's nice!

While chillin' at home
And peering out the window
On a hot summer's day
Just listening to the wind blow

The Mercedes in the driveway
And a bank full of money
All the comforts of home

So rich it's not funny
All these things are cool
But love, children and a wife
That's nice, that's nice!

Like ribbons in the sky
Like reunite' on ice
Love, children and a wife
That's nice, that's nice!

While sitting by a lake
Like drinking a thick chocolate shake
I said Love, children and a wife
That's nice, that's nice!

Many thoughts will excite you
And fill you with glee
When you awaken in the morning
You'll say I'm glad to be me

So to all the good brothers
Repeat after me
Yes, Love, children and a wife
That's nice, that's nice!

A Champion

A Poem of Inspiration

What's in a dream
But a shadow of hope
It's like believing in yourself
When you feel you can't cope

You know you must go on
Never willing to surrender
You must believe you're a champ
And not a pretender

A hero is not someone
To just admire and follow
He's also a person
Whose pride must be swallowed

So hands up to the heavens
All hail to his might
You'll win the last round
With a left and a right

Dig deeper and deeper
And unearth the great prize
That passion for living
It's just the right size

The Wonders of Life

A Poem of Self-Introspection
Imagine you awaken
To a shrill in the night
Something so wondrous
It's sure to delight

You say to yourself
Am I dreaming, I feel
It's too good to be true
It must be surreal

You cast your eyes upward
To a wondrous sight
A vision of loveliness
So bold and so bright

It's kind of like watching
A lady so fair
She flows like a river
With water so clear

A miracle of creation
From our father above
It's his way of saying
I give you my love

A rainbow, an eclipse,
A crackling of light
Some of the things
Not meant to excite

All these forces of nature
Just get stronger with time
They open the doorway
To wonders sublime

Yet Still, I Pray

A Poem Perseverance

I was sitting around pondering
Just the other day
That life is but a mystery
Yet still, I pray

It's one great puzzle
And the pieces won't fit
I just keep trying and trying
I just can't quit

The answers won't come
I'm tired of the struggle
That old 9 – 5
It's too much to juggle

I've given my heart
I've given my soul
That beauteous memory
With a heart too cold

She's taken my inspiration
She's shaken my emotions
Never again
Her name won't be spoken

I say to you brothers
About that sister whose rap
Avoid it like the plaque
You know It's a trap

So to all good people
When I'm lost in the fray
Life might seem hopeless
Yet Still, I Pray

14

Wait

A Poem of Tribulation

I was meditating about my life
And what seemed to be my fate
I had a lot of problems
And they carried enormous weight

I knew I must get busy
And carry out my plan
A masterful creation
About my fellowship to man

The kinds of responsibility
I felt I couldn't shoulder
While they increase in size and shape
Now me, I just get older

I knelt my head in prayer
And called out to our father
I didn't quite understand him
So I quipped why should I bother

He's busy creating blessings
And signing all those checks
So whimsically I turned my back
And said, "I'll wait that's just respect"

My brothers may beseech me
My sisters frown on sight
But still I love our father
I pray both day and night

I pray and pray and pray some more
And call his holy name
Because Jehovah God, Our Father
He loves me just the same!!!

On High

A Poem of Celebration

I had something happen
Just the other day
I awakened abruptly
No words could I say

It sped through my senses
So fast I felt dizzy
It said "Get up my good brother"
"Get up and get busy"

A lot of preparation
Lots of work to be done
A table to be set
For the father and son

A magnificent feast
Must be laid out and spread
To make sure that our brethren
Will surely be fed

To all the people we know
Let's send out a call
So all of our family
Will fill the great hall

It's a time of rejoicing
A time to give praise
So all that feel sadness
Will finally be raised

From the smallest children
To the loftiest high
We'll all be together
By and by

Put on your best clothing
We'll break out the chalice
There'll be a great party
At the royalty's palace

A pauper, a poet, a prophet, a king
Each one on his own
A present to bring

With ultimate favor
I say from my heart
I'll see you tomorrow
From dawn until dark

I'm Free

A Poem About Persistence

Have you ever felt suppressed
Like you've no air to breathe
It's a deep rooted concept
very hard to conceive

You feel like a prisoner
With no hope for tomorrow
You open your heart
But see nothing but sorrow

As you walk down the street
And gaze all around
You look for a friend
But there's none to be found

You've looked in the churches
You've looked in the stores
You've even looked in places
You've never been before

While becoming disenchanted
And feeling unworthy
Just remember to persist
And not become surly

So I say to all people
When there's nothing to see
Just remember your blessing
I'm free, I'm free

Refreshed

A Poem of Rejoicing

When's the last time
You passed every test
Everything was going right
And you'd given your best

You started your day
With a song and a smile
A kiss from your mate
And a hug from your child

You went about your day
With no secrets to hide
A heart full of gladness
And a chest full of pride

When approached for the answer
Instead of feeling compressed
I've got Jehovah in my life
And I'm feeling Refreshed

Inside Out

A Poem of Reflection

Imagine for a moment
Your soul ripped from your body
Your minds a total wreck
You're broken and shoddy

You can't see where you're going
You're blind as a bat
Try as you may
You don't know where you're at

I once had confidence
Things were glowing and pure
Life was breathtaking
And full of allure

I'm going to get it back
I'll work my fingers to the bone
Twenty – four seven
I'll be on the phone

I'll reach deep within me
And uncover that treasure
All the things to unleash
Without any measure

Although so deep
Impossible it seems
I'm Inside Out
And I'm living my dream

Imagination

A Poem of mental Expression

Where is this new place
Called the imagination
It's filled with hope
And ultimate elevation
There is no deceit
There is no frustration
There is no rivalry
And no humiliation
Everyone who exists there
Has the ability to achieve
Their ultimate glory
Anything they conceive
So when travelling abroad
Or through all of creation
If asked where're you going
To my imagination
It's paved with gold
It'll set you on fire
Everything will be great
to your heart's desire
So open your mind
Prepare for the sensation
Get ready for life's best
In your imagination

Silhouette

A Poem About Rapture

While dreaming a dream
And wishing on a star
A virtuous vision
On the horizon afar
I envisioned her features
As clear as could be
Along with the sunlight
She shone down on me
With a magnificent aura
Unspoiled by life
Free from subjection
A gentleman's delight
Too fragile to hold
Yet beckoning to the sight
The length of her character
Reaches staggering heights
As she appears in the distance
With each passing day
I anticipate her next calling
But I know she can't stay
As the din of the night
Becomes awesome to view
Once again I have lost her
Until she comes once anew
Although it's unassuming
And impossible to obtain
I will treasure her memory
With priceless refrain
Silhouette

A Vision Named Heather

A Poem of Familiarity

While strolling down the street
One bright sunny day
What did I see
Walking my way
I didn't know her name
Or if she would even reply
So I got up the courage
And just said "Hi"
"Hello my fair lady
And how do you do"
She shocked me and replied
"I'm fine and you"
She had beautiful brown eyes
With hair like satin-silk
And the prettiest skin
Like carnation milk
Whenever I think
I've something smart to say
She says "Don't try it my good brother
or I'll ruin your day
So like a true virtuoso
I'll just keep it together
And always give respect
To A Vision named Heather

That's Deep

A Poem of Emotional Satire

Have you ever been confronted
With unbearable pain
The kind of immeasurable feeling
That makes you insane

It travels from your forehead
To the tips of your toes
All around your back
And it never slows

It goes down your spine
And all through your heart
Nothing is forgiven
It'll pull you apart

An emotion such as hate
Is consuming like fire
It will turn you inside out
And drain your desire

I've felt it before
It's nothing to recover
I intend to subdue it
Like an insatiable lover

I discovered by chance
An invaluable elixir
I carry it daily
It's my permanent transfixer

Love is the answer
It's free for the talking
It will solve the world's problems
And save all the forsaken

Try it for yourself
You won't be disappointed
Join the ranks of the legion
Of the truly anointed

Once Forgotten

A Poem of Inheritance

There once was an heir
Full of charm and charisma
He fell in and out of love
Quite like an enigma

More often than not
He filed through his treasures
He kept track of them all
In high meticulous ledgers

We're talking about friendships
Folk held high in esteem
All the glorious affairs
Mostly found in your dreams

People dare say
He's lost in the abyss
But I'm back with compassion
Not merely amiss

I've learned a hard lesson
You can't change the past
Always believe in yourself
It's your only true task

Ode To Jehovah

A Poem of Continuance

There's something inside
Just aching to get out
It's an unfettered feeling
That says shout, shout, shout

Sometimes it's hot
And unbearable to touch
The sensation it stirs
Rekindles so much

There are flashes of brilliance
And events out of focus
I feel like a magician
Without hocus-pocus

While going through life
I oft times wonder
Why when I'm lost
He responds with his thunder

Problems and crises|
They come by the bunch
The love of Jehovah
Is there in a crunch

I've gone through the wilderness
Through all situations
I keep close to our father
He knows all implications

So when the sun sets each day
And I question tomorrow
With heavenly promise
I don't beg, steal or borrow

The price of faith
Has no cost to be paid
To be faithful to Jehovah
Is the price in spades

Resurrection 1

A Poem of Rebirth

One day while praying
I felt some respite
All of a sudden
I was cast in the light
It's source was a mystery
And held me in awe
Flashes of brilliance
I never witnessed before
First there was emptiness
Yet as I continued to gaze
Visions of grandeur
Burst through the haze
There were all kinds of glory
An army without end
Bringing miracles and bounty
With serfs to attend
While descending the staircase
Along with the crowd
There was little ole me
Praising out loud
Gone was all sickness
Gone was despair
Until all in the midst
Were filled with great cheer
I held my arms open
And exclaimed with delight
Our father above proclaimed
"Everything was alright"
Suffice to say my spirit's asleep
Yet I know in my heart my soul he will keep
Today is the 1st day of the rest of my life
Thank you Jehovah for protection from strife!

10/4/2007

The Road

A Poem of Presumption

As I was sitting on my porch
And watching life pass me by
I had a cognition
That was hard to deny
While the faces on the on-goers
Kept changing by the second
My station in life
Remained motionless, I reckon
Every once in a while
Someone stopped for a chat
Nothing long or involved
They just asked "where you at?"
"What's going on my friend"
"How're you doing. Where have you been?"
I said, "I'm alright
Now don't ask me again"
I exclaimed with apology
"No harm intended
It's been a long time
Since I've been befriended"
I quickly discovered with self-introspection
Don't be shallow and chaste with gloom and neglect
When opportunity arrives in front of your door
Get up and get going with cheer galore
In order to seize what's coming to you
Be ready to travel into the new
You can't stop progress, life won't wait so be ready
Keep your sights focused on the positive be steady, be steady

Congeniality

A Poem of Compatibility
You've come from my past
To my present and future
You've helped heal my wounds
Like some gold laced sutures

I'm talking about healing
Things applied to old legends
Mixtures and potions
Fast churning not dredging

When we were young children
And just running around
I reflect back on those moments
A great friend to astound

So here we are today
Charles and D.C.
Where do we go from here
It remains to be seen

Let's put our heads to the sky
And cherish moments that come
We'll achieve both our dreams
We've only begun Congeniality

Revelation

A Poem of Destiny

Somedays when I awaken
It seems like it's a dream
With cash and substance and love galore
A man of many dreams

Since this is not my actual case
It's what I'd like to be
I have a lot of people
With help and support for me

Some people say that life's a trip
And it's only what you make it
My reply to them is "Toughen Up"
Be real you sure can't fake it

Wealth and fame and health and love
Are signs of sure prosperity
So I would like to say for sure
I'll win It's called security

I'll work and pray and love and strive
And seek all princely goals
With help from family, friends and God
True wealth be mine untold

Jah Love

A Poem of Divine Emotional Protection

I was prophesying about my life
Of things I'd like to be
A wealthy, energetic, healthy man
One everyone yearns to see

When I was in the prime of my life
And fortune filled my dreams
Each day I woke to happiness
No worries, so it seemed

When I was young and still naïve
With a heart so easily broken
All it took was a little love
And lies so easily spoken

When disappointment set in my soul
And I turned my back to our father
My heart caused me to feel despair
Why live? No. Why should I bother?

I cried and moaned and felt self-pity
Like no man has ever known
But still our heavenly father loved me
Thank God how much I've grown

I now know without a shred of doubt
I'm someone to be loved
I believe I have some friends on earth
As well as on high above

When fear or sickness or poverty or pain
Begin to rear their ugly heads
I will call upon our father
His love will heal instead

So the message building within my soul
It's impressive from the start
I'll always love myself and others
My God, He's in my heart!

Faith

A Poem Sensory Delight

What is faith
But a layer of hope
It'll fill your body
With unlimited scope

It's like parkay butter
So silky and smooth
Every fiber and crevice
Every lining and groove

Now there's grey poupon spread
Paprika and spice
All kinds of additives
For palate delight

All these preparations
Cannot even compare
To the feeling of Faith
It's all too rare

Like the rarest diamond
A most admirable sight
It gets better with time
It increases each night

It comes for Jehovah
Who created us all
When we draw near to our father
We shall never fall

Faith is unrelenting
But available at will
Just reach to the high heavens
It's the ultimate thrill

When we abide by his calling
Life is pleasing to live
Our father is open
To whatever we give

So I close this heart message
With a resounding yes, yes, yes
With our pulse on our faith
We will always be blessed!!!

Father oh father
I stand at your door
I will always love you
As you've loved me before

Signs

A Poem of Direction

As I was sitting at my desk
And examining my situation
Ideas kept popping in my head
Of relative propitiation

Which bills should I pay first and when
What manner to execute them
How in the world can you pay bills
When your mind says just refute them

While creditors just keep piling up
And basics become a chore
I know the answer's in keeping faith
It's never failed before

I keep receiving heavenly help
As well as help on earth
People seem to know my plight
Thank God it sure can't hurt

I'm finding money on the ground
Just change though small in count
While big money comes in little spurts
It's honest money, money that I fount

I've got a 9-5 to help me pay my fellow man
Yet still I ask our father, please
Show me your master-plan

A plan which has the ways and means
To increase my financial prosperity
So I can once again live well
With confidence and self-clarity

Luck and love and fun and life
Are commodities to cherish
I always strive to be real wise
So that all I do will flourish

So I ask you Jehovah God
Humbly and with much respect
Keep giving me signs of love and wealth
So bills remain in check!!!

Suitable Attire

A Poem of Grace

There once was a man
Of Suitable Attire
He was very debonair
With thoughts to inspire When going about town
At the hottest locales
Whether with friends
Or the prettiest femme fatales

He had the kind of charisma
That would excite a small crowd
To see him at work
Would make any man proud

To befriend him was priceless
To mimic quite true
What was given most freely
Was by far quite cool

When stepping out in style
Quite dapper to see
Everyone surely knew
It's the man known as Mr. B.

My objective quite personal
Is to be all I can be
With my head firmly on my shoulder
The world shall see!!!

He's Got His Hands On Me

A Poem of Divine Empowerment

I was feeling kind of down
About my present impropriety
At times I tend to forget
He's got his hands on me

I'm talking about our father
Who created the heavens and the sea
He's magnificent and all mighty
And he's got his hands on me

I need him in my life
Like oxygen to breathe
He's oh so awesome
And he's got his hands on me

He put the stars in the sky
He taught the birds how to fly
There's nothing he can't do
And he's got his hands on me

So with much reverence and respect
I reflect as you see
My problems are infinitesimal, since
He's got his hands on me

I once had divine favor
Everything shined gloriously
I loved his spiritual touch, And
He's got his hands on me

He may not be my doctor
He may not be my chief
But he'll always be my savior, because
<u>He's Got His Hands On Me</u>

The Legion of Spiritual Soldiers

A Poem of Social Security

I've been inspired to recruit some good men
Some good women, some good children, all to be friends
A cavalcade of soldiers with talents without question
Abilities often found in a world class equestrian

We shall all come together to help all mankind
To generate goodwill with intensity profound
We'll fight the good fight to bring forth prosperity
Our final objective collective security

We'll travel near and far over difficult receptacles
Our travels will be treacherous filled with unexpected spectacles
In spite of such hardships with no rest in sight
We'll stay true to our course and proceed day and night

A shilling, a sixpence, a dollar, a yen
Though small in value we need them to spend
I surmise we all need money though virtue is best
We must pursue group validity, we persist no less

Teachers, doctors, laborers it doesn't matter
Let's all come together to share that great platter
A plate filled with our hopes and our dreams
Our menu is full, not lacking not lean

WE must proceed together so we'll all reign on high
Let's gather our goods and services and pray to survive
We must pray together and grow bolder and bolder
Our ultimate goal to be Spiritual Soldiers

The Spiritual Fire

A Poem of Spiritual Fortitude

Things are getting rough
When I sleep, I perspire
Why am I so hot
It's because of Spiritual Fire

What I'm talking about is complicated
There's all kinds of connotations
All types of problems
And no sign of any meaningful congratulations

On the phone, in the mail
And even in my head
They're all real manifestations
The kind most people dread

At times I walk around
Feeling lost without hope
And then it hits me
Of course I can cope

I'll get out of this shell, I'll get out of this rut
Our father is calling I must get in touch
He's got all the answers, he's always on time
A billion for a billion, his record's sublime

The fire of pain is not scorching to feel
But it's weight is tremendous, I'll be humble and kneel
Our father will deliver me, I'll ask for his help
I'll also ask him to help others and not just myself

Whether I'm weary, downtrodden or sick
My response will be rapid, poignant and quick
When my burdens try to accumulate
And attempt to drag me under
I'll lord back with laughter
And release on high thunder

So I'll close this passage to all who'll receive
If you open your hearts gladly, you'll get a reprieve
A pardon, so to speak, from our Spiritual Sire
He'll always guide us safely through <u>The Spiritual Fire</u>

Just Passing By

A Poem of Disenchantment

While reflecting on a moment of emotional magic
A thought kept responding, quite dim but still tragic
A tale of two hearts united but separate
One was quite sturdy and the other one eclectic

While he knew his heart and moreso his emotions
He searched for his true love, not just a mere token
Now check for an instant the lady in question
When speaking of true love it's just a minute suggestion

Each one on their own pursuing a feeling
Her heart's set in stone his mind keeps on reeling
Although he once knew true love a thought from the past
Pursuing this diva is futility aghast

Maybe not intentional but sordid no less
Her emotions were flighty like an overnight guest
Now keeping in perspective all relative nuances
A lady of leisure embodies all self-truancies

So I say from experience always lead with your mind
If you lead with your heart what you receive won't be kind
In fairness to the ladies who choose independence
It's only right they always crave to have resplendence

So to all of you fellas who seek the best mate
You should always begin with that 1st just friend date
Then if you find you're not her ultimate guy
She told you from jump that she's Just Passing By

A Miracle on Central Ave.

A Poem of Heavenly Expectation

This is a tale of a man for all seasons
He cavorted around town for all kinds of reasons
People would gossip so thick you could hear it
The man in their mouths with the unbreakable spirit

This was a priestly man and more often than not
I may not be what you're looking for but I'm all that you got
I'm a pioneer of sorts imbedded with cheer
I'm fixated on the positive the sign says "Road Ahead Clear"

I'm seeking the lord and our heavenly host
They always give favor to whom needs them the most
I'm searching the world over for spiritual emancipation
I'll attend every class for the heavenly equation

I'm yearning to escape that prison without walls
It's that place in the mind that won't answer the call
A spiritual ghetto filled with delusions and graft
No future, no vision, no unity, no craft

From the room where I sit and pray all day long
The message comes through loudly keep going, be strong
No matter how silent, no matter how still
I know he will deliver me, he will, he will!

No Strings Attached

A Poem of True Affinity

What do you call it when your heart's all a flutter?
It's like that huge mansion on the hill with nary a shutter
When you receive your heart's desire free of charge
When you run the political office for the councilman-at-large

Imagine for a moment that you just won the lottery
Imagine that raving beauty was once making pottery
The unexpected occurrences that became everyday events
that once healthy, wealthy man who has hardly a cent

What I'm leading up to are the realistic goals
The ones we all dream of achieving before we get old
Like who expects diamonds & caviar, nothing more &nothing less

When you go to <u>On High</u> and experience the summit
All things so fantastic nothing stays in your stomach
After this happens you'll feel that life is a breeze
You'll feel just like being mellow with your main squeeze

Apparitions once pricey and necessary for self-value
Are being replaced with cash and carry, how true, how true
So when learning to do things so you're really relaxed
Give freely cause it's right with <u>No Strings Attached!</u>

Transformation

A Poem of Spiritual Augmentation

I must relate a story of spiritual augmentation
It's a tale of a young lad who dreamed of ultimate appreciation
No matter how much he prayed to be loved by his peers
His emotions remained in limbo as he realized his worst fears

Although you may give and give and hunger to belong
Sometimes things just aren't meant to be so continue and be strong
Although the path in life is shrouded and often filled with doubt
You must continue on your path to gain your hidden clout

Yes your credibility grows and increases day by day
You cannot measure spiritual wealth based on what other people say
I have learned that lasting wealth is given if you just pursue it
Once you find its' hidden source guess
what you'll be drawn right to it

Money, jewels and material riches may shine
but you should stop and ponder
Just when you think you've got it all, there's more just over yonder
To be a glutton and always yearn for more, is considered to be a sin
Never being satisfied will wear your spirit thin

I now realize to be thankful is gracious and a blessing
So I'll keep praying to Jehovah and let other's keep impressing
I know what trail to blaze on earth and what path to blaze in heaven
I'll laugh and share and grow today just like when I was seven

I want to communicate to our guides in heaven
As well as my friends on earth
Our father has given me his plans so no longer do I search
I know I have the skills as well as the ability of configuration
Now all I need is your support and help to
complete my <u>Transformation!</u>

On High Revisited

A Poem Domicile Affinity

I often have a dream about a place called "On High"
It doesn't even exist yet but it will if we all try
Its' location is a secret one I'm meant to discover
It's a sparkle, in my mind, with faith I'll uncover

A mansion, a villa, a condo, a chateau
It's a realistic place where all spiritual people will go
They will convene at this address for comfort and great pleasure
Their ultimate desires and appointments in ledgers

I hope I will live there in the last days of my life
I'll reside there with my family, my children, my wife
We'll surround it with an aura and the best security money can buy
We'll pray daily, to Jehovah, so all included will thrive

I have this clear vision though small and minute
I believe that with faith all will make the commute
There will be ample space and all will be welcome inside
When they see what we have built they'll be bursting with pride

We will have built a small monument to our father Jehovah
A facility built with great toil like The White Cliffs of Dover
It's but one component of the complex called "Rise"
Once embarking on this journey all will receive a great prize

My call is to all people regardless of race
Regardless of life's station, regardless of pace
You don't have to fast just adherent to God's will
We'll reach this common objective and remember to kneel

Artisans, professionals, blue collar and seniors
All keeping faith focused through the prosperous and the lean years
Masterpieces, fingerpaintings and caricatures unfinished
Storebins of plenty so bursting replenished

I've heard stories of hell but mostly heaven on earth
Inspire me to always reach higher for spiritual rebirth
Whether thanking Jehovah or drying our eyes
Lets look forward to convening at our home at <u>On High</u>

My Guardian

A Poem of Spiritual Self Portrait

I keep getting these visions of great times from long ago
The times when people were friendly and would always say hello
Even though times were tough and we worked for every penny
That great lady, who brought me up, always
saved some space for many

We sometimes ate tender bitters with some ketchup and some syrup
Man I tell you it tasted so good like it was
cooked by a pink faced cherub
I struggled through my early years but I always seemed so cheerful
The love Alverta, gave to me, still makes me glad and tearful

Some may think it strange to think back on the past
But where would we be today if we forgot old feelings cast
I use those values, she instilled in me and thank her everyday
I may not show it to everyone but thank God how much I pray

As time passed by each day and life eased as I grew older
I know my spiritual fortitude helped as I grew strong and bolder
When sometimes I felt like giving up and becoming mean and defiant
I remembered those old school reprimands so now I'm self-reliant

I kept looking high and looking low for the answer to my dilemma
How can I get more than one free gift,
that only happens in December
Life is only complicated if you follow your own hunches
I have come to know our father well, he sends his aid in bunches

I've been to school, to college and a church of higher education
And yet, just now, I've received a startling cerebral inclination
When searching life for the means to save and protect your very soul
You have to be your 1st line of defense, if not you won't grow old

Not your father, not your mother, not your family or friends
Can bring you to Jehovah
You must be the one who is spiritual or else I'll say I told ya'
Pray and heal and fast and love and you will surely see
When it comes to my own salvation, <u>My Guardian</u>, it's me, it's me, it's me

Bones

A Poem of Physiological Healing

This is a poem of Physiological Healing
One that's forgotten but none the less feeling
By feeling, I mean we need them like bees need honey
I'm talking about bones, like survival needs money
Sometimes I lay awake at night burdened by the pain
I meditate and pray but the result is the same
It keeps naggin' like a surrogate mother
It makes me want to scream and get back under the covers
You know, life can be hurtful but it can also bring great pleasure
You need to be determined like an off shore dredger
You must keep digging and drilling into life's deep dark chasm
How much farther do I go? Well, it's about one long, wide fathom.
When your head hurts, your hands and your back
Not medicine, not vitamins or that preacher named Jack
It's a sin and a shame when there's no cure in sight
Guess what I have learned? Go to Jehovah at night.
Go to a place where you feel safe and secure
The answer is with Jehovah, of this I am sure
When your muscles and tendons and arteries and veins
All feel like they're on fire and you need heavenly restrain
I say from experience and yet say learn for yourself
Jehovah is the answer, his book's on the shelf
Whether physical or spiritual by nature
Faith will melt your problems like an Alaskan glacier
So the next time you're hurting and feeling no one else cares
Take your pains to Jehovah, for your burdens he'll bear
Bones

Resurrection 2

A Poem of Heavenly Re-ignition

I've been having this cognition for a very long time
When I engage this conception the feeling is sublime
A place in my memory that's void of regret
It's luscious and soothing and hard to forget
Imagine my sensation when realizing my luck
I seemed to have been empowered, more like moonstruck
The most beautiful woman would pale in comparison
The comments, would seem shallow, even from Ms. Barrington
I used to mope around, all day, looking for empathy
Every now and again I got short tipped sympathy
People felt sorrow and thus threw me some bones
However when all bets were collected I was there, still alone
I roved around groveling and accepting life's worst
Playing a derelict like a role scripted & rehearsed
I kept lounging around like a hobo that's funny
Like a fragile toy poodle or ever-ready bunny
Then out of the blew like a thunder of lightning
A voice from above so loud it was frightening
"Get up my son, get up and get going
Get going in the direction that your destiny is showing"
"Greatness awaits you but I attest it won't be easy
Go confront all obstacles and prosper, for sheezy
Get rid of the poverty, use all the strength you can muster
Get up and accept your life with glory and luster"
"Recapture your desire to live life to the fullest
Use your God given talents, not violence not bullets"
I look forward to adhering to the will of our father
He's always been right there for me, no diggity, no bother
I'll close this small passage with a heart-felt confession
With god's help I'll defeat the greatest oppression
Poverty, sickness, ignorance and depression
I'm on my way home to Spiritual Resurrection

The Touch of You

A Poem of Heavenly Inoculation

I remember some lyrics from some time ago
I'll script them, here for you, so you'll know
"The Touch of You is Driving Me Out Of My Head"
I would like to think it brings me back to reality instead
Imagine, if you would, something so darn enticing
Something just so good, it's like cake with great icing
You know, like that submarine sandwich with onions and peppers
Like those drop dead gorgeous cheerleaders
or bodylicious hot-steppers
The point I'm trying to relay is mostly in the mind
Things so indescribable it would take a lifetime
Put first and foremost what you would most like to acquire
The finest woman or sharp man, whom you truly desire
I dreamed of a woman, so fly and delicious
I couldn't even think, all her moves were suspicious
She just couldn't be real she embodied so much
I would meditate all day of when we'd once again touch
To see her, was to want her, she had all that I'd need
I would do all that she wanted, whether love her or plead
Be in my life, with you I'm complete
True love and romance, not envy or conceit
It brings thoughts, to my mind, of a biblical story
One, in which they say, Jesus was held high in glory
Just to touch a small piece of his glorious hem
Would inspire you to live proper, not evil, not sin
So to search the world over and find your soul mate
This is tedious, at best, go figure your fate
I mean to heal what was once broken and return to full power
It's like that feeling of love that gets stronger each hour
I've had a lot of chances to reach my emotional peak

57

But something always stopped me, doubt or trechi'c
I keep believing that one day, by trial or by error
Some beautiful lady would say "I love you and I'm yours forever"
It has finally happened and with no speculation
I have someone in my life and I say with great adoration
"I don't need you to promise me gold that accrues"
Why? Because my heart skips a beat at <u>The Touch of You</u>

I'm A Beacon for The Lord

A Poem of Spiritual Illumination

I've just had some cognitions of a supernatural kind
Yes the premonitions I'm having are most easy to find
These thoughts are disturbing since they occur everyday
They are deeply embedded and so I study and pray
I pray to return to the bright day of yore
When I was amazed and inspired by faith galore
Everything that I thought was surrounded by love
Deep rooted in God in the heavens above
My emotions were fragile but none-the-less stable
I searched for brotherly affection unlike Cain + Abel
To be born into a family is a wonderful feeling
But to be close to our father raises hopes to the ceiling
I know to reach Jehovah I must first seek his son
It's a daily progression and my work's never done
Just at the moment I feel I'll never reach my goal
I get unexpected blessings which empower my soul
People used to hurl, at me, insults to defame
I learned to take heed, of God, it's surely no game
To be popular and wealthy are what most people treasure
But the best course, in life, is to be faithful without measure
I've searched for many purposes to get on the right path
I must pursue righteousness to avoid God's wrath
With faith and love I feel really self-assured
I'm ignited on the righteous path and I'm A Beacon for The Lord

Catlaclysm

A Poem of Social Reconstruction

Cataclysm by nature a social upheaval
Marked by emotional, mental and spiritual retrieval
Society is going through a turbulent change
With events marked with indecision and trends rearranged

This period of unrest creates all kinds of depressions
People of all races with enormous pent-up frustrations
We're all in a quandry looking intensely for solutions
Concisely we're looking for leadership not slick talking collusions

I've said it before and I'll say it again
We must come together and stay focused like kin
Be that it may, whether aristocrat or blue-collar
We'll only survive if we all stand together and Holler!!!

Lets not put the blame on the upper class wealthy
Because somewhere down the line it gets negative and unhealthy
Like a rotating filter with degenerative static
It spreads evil, plagues and destruction that's severely erratic

So come ye faithful brethren lets fight the good fight
Put your faith to the forefront so we'll achieve community delight
Instead of severity that strips, kills and maims
Lets commune together since we're all basically the same

Let us be a people of greatness who all bask in the sun
With wealth aplenty for all and praise for
work exceptionally well-done
I'll keep striving to be a messenger who proclaims a message of hope
I'm proud to be of a people who daily face
struggle and cope Cataclysm!!!

I'll Just Start With Me

A Poem of Self Portrait

I've been having daily visions of the man I'd like to be
A man with a depth of character most everyone would love to see
A head of hair so curly, with luster to the root
Vitality unlimited with wealth and charm to boot

I'd love to awaken each day to a fire crackling in the den
A loving wife lounging next to me
With a cup of hot coffee filled right to the brim
She would be so gorgeous, yet kind and fair,
with skin so smooth and clear
Whenever she'd enter any room, I'd sparkle when she drew near

Her name might be Natasha, Bethsheba or maybe Grace or Joan
In any case, what err her name, I'd long for our time alone
I can just imagine two kids, a boy a girl and yes some rare exotic pets
We'd live in our luxurious house, On High,
oh God how good and calm it gets

Now this portrait that I'm painting, I hope someday will surely be
With all the greatest accoutrements, sprung from our family tree
Since this is but a dream I hold, most dearly in my heart
I'll start with my own self-improvement, so
my dreams will be bright not dark

So I'll just continue working to make this dream a reality
I'm sure one day it will come to pass so I'll just Start With Me!!!

No More Sleepless Nights

A poem of Sanctification

I was embarking on a location unknown to me
I felt a tingling, yet soothing sensation
One that's powerful as you will come to see
It seems as though whenever trouble confronts me
And I'm shrouded in unnatural pain
Our father sends me a spiritual message, again and again and again
He reminds me that a problem is but an obstacle
That shall be overcome
This can surely be accomplished as sure as the rising of the sun
Through faith and perseverance I know
my circumstances will change
I believe God will take the ingredients and simply rearrange, them
I've been pursuing the answers haphazardly
Instead of with joy & zeal & zest
I know within my mind, body & soul are all the answers to this test
This is the time to answer the call
Our father has put within my being
With the help of God's supernatural force
All my troubles will just start fleeing
The path before me has become riddled
With unhealthy pain & financial convolution
I'm reaching out to Jehovah God
I know he's my greatest sole solution
I once had the daily favor of God and I prayed regularly thru his son
I'm going to start applying my faith, to my life
My life 's work has just begun

When I was young and restless, God touched me night and day
It seems as I grew older, I got lost within fray
There's no doubt, however, that God is in
control and guides my daily life
I'm going to focus on helping myself and pay
my debts, no games, deceit or fights
So I relinquish, without hesitation, all regrets & past respites
I'll then have some peace on earth and <u>No More Sleepless Nights!!!</u>

Trying To Make A Dollar Out of 99 Cents

A Poem of Financial Futility

There are a few things in life
That just aren't meant to be
I'll inscribe one here for you
Then I'm sure that you will see

And it hurt just like the Dickens
My finances were chaste and wide open
Oft like "easy pickins"

I'd sit around the table all day and all night
Try as I may it just wouldn't come out right
I counted and counted and with my mind turned and spent
I just couldn't make A Dollar Out of 99 cents

You may scoff at me, laugh at me and say he's such a jerk
But just like you I'm determined and continue to work
I keep searching and searching yet the answer's the same
My detractors keep repeating just pay it's simple and plain

When confronting an obstacle and money's real tight
Remember this message and everything will be right
Don't haggle, cynicize, worry or relent
Stop wasting time Trying To Make A Dollar Out of 99 Cents

Priceless

A Poem of Family Fortitude

I must tell a tale of a family reconciliation
It came about by chance on a festive occasion
It was the 4th of July in 2008
It started out slowly but it ended up great
The weather was cloudy there was doubt all amiss
My family was waiting we'd avoid a bad triste
Myself and some friends, seven in total
We anticipated fun at the back-yard social
We engaged in some shopping our spirits were high
We intended to get B-B-Q and apricot pies
Instead we settled for chicken and drinks for the palate
We got plenty of cups and a nice tossed green salad
Our method of travel was shaky at best
We never got sullen we stayed cheerful no less
As we arrived at the picnic the magnificent seven
The welcome we got felt like something from heaven
The kids were elated my sister was happy
I hate to admit it I was tearful and sappy
As we all settled down and made group introductions
Materializing in our presence positive old family repercussions
Happiness love and deep feelings replenished
We set about preparing the fun food undiminished
Now in the process of setting the grill
Guess what started to happen, It was raining, how ill
Now here starts the tale of how my pride grew to the hilt
My sister said "Let's party" no matter how tilt
All the children were doubtful all the adults were amazed
Yet me and my sister continued unfazed
So what do you think happened as we prepared our tradition
The rain began to cease and we praised our decision
Everyone popped up happy and we ate all the food to the bone
We had music and fireworks and also about 20 folks strong

We had burgers and chicken and hot-dogs and buns
We had chips and all kinds of beverages and laughter and fun
Yes, we even had a small fireworks display but yet best of all
I played with the children no matter how big or how small
I caught myself thinking how great this would be
If our father would bless me continuously
So I'm closing this message with thoughts for the future
I pray to regain my prominence as a credible tutor
My family and my friends are invaluable, indeed
What's their value to me, why they're all 10th degree

Supernatural

A Poem of Positive Spiritual Evolvement

I'm being drawn to a power beyond my comprehension
It seems to emanate from an entity with unlimited ascension
It's as if Jehovah has sent me an advisor as a heavenly host
He's always right there for me when I need him the most
My task that I have accepted is enormous I know
Yet I've set my sights on it's completion so my mentality must grow
I may need to return to academic days of yore
Or maybe pursue professional horizons I've never tried before
The masterplan is written the directions are plain
So I must begin constructing the responsibilities again
I'll start with my own education so my peers, friends and kin
Will once again listen and support my regimen
The ultimate project though difficult and lengthy
Will be worthwhile for all and we'll end up with plenty
As I pursue the building of the project call "Rise"
I need spiritual guidance to achieve this great prize
While my supporter's on earth give motivation and approval
I sometimes get discouraged and thus need negative removal
Much literature is arriving from local indications
Yet I also receive contacts from international affiliations
So I'm going to heighten my level of comprehension
And hope and pray for earthly and spiritual retention
To obtain the ability to relay to my fellow constituents
That we all must educate ourselves to obtain future unprecedents
So I'm rolling up my sleeves and breaking out my boots
I'm pulling out all stops and investing my loot
To all those who say it cannot be done I say "Au con traire"
I've got the blessing of Jehovah and that's Supernatural

Author's Challenge

I am formally issuing this personal challenge to all like minded individuals, who at one point in their lives felt that they couldn't go on. They had given up hope and believed no one understood their problems and circumstances and there was no help available to them.

I have come to know, that through Christian experience, faith is the ultimate answer. It goes without saying that as a person blessed by God, I was given the faith to continue living and re-instilled with the desire to be a good person intent on being a positive force in society.

Speaking from my own life experiences, as a blessed person, I have to testify that the spiritual force that oversees us all has chosen me as but one person who can make a positive, constructive and beneficial difference in society. I am no better than anyone else but I know because of the things I feel and understand, I must accept my mission, from our father Jehovah God, to be but one vehicle to spread his message of love for all people (mankind) and relay a spiritual purpose to pursue accurate knowledge of his holy word, worldwide.

I assert respectively, that my expressing our creator's name as Jehovah God, is due to my Christian upbringing (Baptist church) and personal acceptance but I do not minimize anyone else's acceptance of our heavenly father's name whatever you accept it to be. Glory to our father in heaven.

I only want to express a spiritual commonality that we all share as human beings on this planet we call earth. I only wish to represent my heartfelt thanks, to our spiritual father, for re-instilling within me the desire to be humble. Humble enough to desire to serve others again and seek out like minded spiritual people with similar aspirations.

I believe that a great deal of people need an outlet for their goals, needs and desires and I strive to be just one such person. A person who will listen and help them achieve whatever reasonable goals which they may have.

In spite of locale, age, nationality, religion, profession, physicality or level of education, I believe that everyone has something to offer. Lets come together to help each other to develop a foundation whose primary concern is to be a haven for the eradication of all affiliated supporters problems. By recruiting the proper qualified professionals, we the associated constituents will achieve our life goals. We shall recruit the required doctors, lawyers, business advisors, architects, engineers, laborer and all necessary staff needed to make this complex and foundation a reality.

I also believe that despite the seemingly enormity of this project, if there is a need for it and if we pray on it, with Jehovah's blessing, it will happen. Nothing being overlooked or taken for granted, lets come together in his holy name.

Thank you for your support and may Jehovah God bless us.

Sincerely,

Charles A. Barner

Personal Approval

Amen!!

Society Response

Notes – Comments – Suggestions
(Sign, date & return as soon as possible)
(Optional)

_____   _____   _____

Name   Address   Date

Phone No. (   )_____

Email: _____

Printed in the United States
By Bookmasters